interchange

THIRD EDITION

Jack C. Richards
with *Jonathan Hull* and *Susan Proctor*

WORKBOOK 1 B

CAMBRIDGE UNIVERSITY PRESS
Cambridge, New York, Melbourne, Madrid, Cape Town, Singapore, São Paulo

Cambridge University Press
40 West 20th Street, New York, NY 10011–4211, USA

www.cambridge.org
Information on this title: www.cambridge.org/9780521601795

First published 2005
6th printing 2005

Interchange Third Edition Workbook 1B has been developed from *New Interchange* Workbook 1B,
first published by Cambridge University Press in 1997.

Printed in Hong Kong, China

ISBN-13   978-0-521-60179-5 Workbook
ISBN-10   0-521-60179-7 Workbook

Art direction, book design, photo research, and layout services: Adventure House, NYC

Contents

Acknowledgments

Illustrations

Rob De Bank 90
Tim Foley 52 (*top*)
Travis Foster 70
Randy Jones 49, 51, 52 (*bottom*), 66, 72, 73, 78, 79, 86, 95

Ben Shannon 50
Dan Vasconcellos 53, 91, 92
Sam Viviano 54, 69, 77

Photo credits

55 (*clockwise from left*) © Getty Images; © Masterfile; © Corbis/Sygma
56 © Blair Seitz/Photo Researchers
57 (*clockwise from top left*) © Doug Armand/Getty Images; © Ken Straiton/Corbis; © Ned Gillette/Corbis; © Gary Landsman/Corbis; © Jon Riley/Getty Images; © Viviane Moos/Corbis
59 (*left to right*) © Michael Goldman/Getty Images; © Robert A. Issacs/Photo Researchers; © Hoa-Qui/Getty Images; © Frederick McKinney/Getty Images
60 © Alamy
61 (*top to bottom*) © Will & Deni McIntyre/Getty Images; © Zefa London/Corbis
62 (*left to right*) © Richard Passmore/Getty Images; © EPA/David G. McIntyre/AP/Wide World Photos; © Wonderfile
63 (*top to bottom*) © Joe Cornish/Stone/Getty Images; © Eric Sander/Getty Images
64 (*left to right*) © Gavin Hellier/Getty Images; © Jeffrey Sylvester/Getty Images; © Alexis Duclos/Getty Images
65 © Noboru Komine/Photo Researchers

71 © Bruce Ayers/Getty Images
74 (*top to bottom*) © Matthew Klein/Photo Researchers; © Peter Johansky/Getty Images; © Roy Morsch/Corbis; © Karen Leeds/Corbis; © Alan Bergman/Getty Images
76 (*top to bottom*) © Larry Gatz/Getty Images; © Wonderfile; © Brian Leatart/Foodpix
80 © Travelpix/Getty Images
81 (*left to right*) © Guido Alberto Rossi/Getty Images; © Bob Abraham/Pacific Stock; © A & L Sinibaldi/Getty Images
82 (*top to bottom*) © Dennis Puleston/Photo Researchers; © Robert W. Hernandez/Photo Researchers
83 (*top to bottom*) © Ken Fisher/Getty Images; © Telegraph Colour Library/Getty Images; © Wolfgang Kaehler/Getty Images; © Karl Weidman/Photo Researchers; © Donovan Reese/Getty Images
93 (*left to right*) © L.D. Gordon/Getty Images; © Ariel Skelley/Corbis; © John Henly/Corbis
94 © Superstock
96 © Getty Images

9 What does she look like?

1 *Write the opposites. Use the words in the box.*

☐ light   ☑ straight   ☐ young   ☐ short   ☐ tall

1. curly / *straight*   4. long / _____
2. dark / _____   5. short / _____
3. elderly / _____

2 *Descriptions*

A Match the words in columns A and B. Write the descriptions.

A	B	
☑ dark	☐ aged	1. *dark brown*
☐ fairly	☑ brown	2. _____
☐ good	☐ height	3. _____
☐ medium	☐ long	4. _____
☐ middle	☐ looking	5. _____

B Answer the questions using the descriptions from part A.

1. A: What does he look like?

   B: *He's good-looking.* _____

2. A: How long is his hair?

   B: _____

3. A: What color is his hair?

   B: _____

4. A: How old is he?

   B: _____

5. A: How tall is he?

   B: _____

3 **Complete this conversation with questions.**

Steve: Let's find Amy. I need to talk to her.

Jim: _What does she look like?_ _____

Steve: She's quite pretty, with straight black hair.

Jim: And _____

Steve: It's medium length.

Jim: _____

Steve: She's fairly tall.

Jim: And _____

Steve: She's in her early twenties.

Jim: _____

Steve: Sometimes. I think she's wearing them now.

Jim: I think I see her over there. Is that her?

4 **Describe yourself. How old are you? What do you look like?
What are you wearing today?**

_____

_____

_____

_____

_____

5 Circle two things in each description that do not match the picture.
Then correct the information.

George

1. George is in his (late sixties). He's pretty tall.
   He has a mustache, and he's bald.
   He's wearing a shirt, jeans, and boots.

   He isn't in his late sixties. He's in his twenties.

   _____

   _____

   _____

2. Sophie is about 25. She's very pretty.
   She's medium height. Her hair is long and blond.
   She's wearing a black sweater, a jacket, and tennis shoes.
   She's standing next to her motorcycle.

   _____

   _____

   _____

   _____

Sophie

Lucinda

3. Lucinda is in her early twenties.
   She's pretty serious-looking. She has glasses.
   She's fairly tall, and has curly dark hair.
   She's wearing a nice-looking jacket and jeans.

   _____

   _____

   _____

   _____

6

Which of these clothing items are more formal? Which are more casual? Complete the chart.

scarf   boots   necktie

skirt

T-shirt

suit

shorts   cap   running shoes

shirt

dress

jeans

Formal	Casual
shirt	

7

Write a sentence about each person. Use the words in the box and participles.

Mandy

Edward and Kate

William

Giorgio   Alice

☑ man   ☐ carry a jacket
☐ woman   ☐ wear sunglasses
☐ one   ☑ stand next to Alice
☐ ones   ☐ talk to the man
☐ tall woman   ☐ wear a suit and tie

1. *Giorgio is the man standing next to Alice.*

2. _____

3. _____

4. _____

5. _____

8 *Answer the questions. Use the words given.*

Ken   Carlos   Jake   Marie   Dan   Cindy   Angela

1. A: Which ones are Jake and Marie?

   B: *They're the ones playing cards.*   (playing cards)

2. A: Who's Carlos?

   B: _____   (couch)

3. A: Who are Dan and Cindy?

   B: _____   (dancing)

4. A: Which one is Angela?

   B: _____   (couch)

5. A: Who's Ken?

   B: _____   (short black hair)

---

9 *Rewrite these sentences and questions.*
Find another way to say them using the words given.

1. A: Who's Mika?

   Which one's Mika?   (Which)

   B: She's the one in the black dress.

   She's the one wearing the black dress.   (wearing)

2. A: Which ones are the teachers?

   _____   (Who)

   B: They're the ones on the couch.

   _____   (sitting)

3. A: Which one is Larry?

   _____   (Who)

   B: He's the guy wearing the coat.

   _____   (in)

10 *Complete this description. Use the present continuous or the participle of the verbs in the box.*

☐ ask   ☐ carry   ☑ look   ☐ stand   ☐ use   ☐ wait   ☐ walk   ☐ wear

Yeah, classes start tomorrow. What am I doing? Let's see . . . . I *'m looking* _____ out my window right now. There's a middle-aged woman _____ her dog, and a young guy _____ the pay phone. Two people _____ next to him. Hey! The one _____ a baseball hat is my classmate! Some people _____ at the bus stop. A serious-looking woman _____ for directions. And hey, here comes a really cute girl _____ a backpack. Wait a minute! I know her. That's my old girlfriend. I have to go now! Bye.

11 *Choose the correct responses.*

1. A: Where's Jan?

   B: *She couldn't make it.* _____

   ■ I'd like to meet her.
   ■ She couldn't make it.

2. A: Who's Sam?

   B: _____

   ■ I'm afraid I missed him.
   ■ The handsome guy near the door.

3. A: Is she the one on the couch?

   B: _____

   ■ That's right.
   ■ Let's see.

4. A: How tall is she?

   B: _____

   ■ Fairly long.
   ■ Pretty short.

10 Have you ever ridden a camel?

1 **Match the verb forms in columns A and B.**

A	B
1. be _d_	a. gone
2. call ____	b. done
3. do ____	c. seen
4. eat ____	✓d. been
5. go ____	e. called
6. have ____	f. jogged
7. jog ____	g. made
8. make ____	h. had
9. see ____	i. tried
10. try ____	j. eaten

2 **Complete the questions in these conversations. Use the present perfect of the verbs in Exercise 1.**

1. A: _Have you seen_ the new Keanu Reeves movie?

   B: Yes, it's very good.

2. A: _____ running lately?

   B: Yes, Sue usually runs in the morning and evening.

3. A: How many phone calls _____ lately?

   B: I made only one – on my father's birthday.

4. A: How long _____ those sunglasses?

   B: I've had them for a few weeks.

5. A: _____ at Rio Café?

   B: Yes, we've already eaten there. It's very good but
      a little expensive.

6. A: How many times _____ shopping
      at the mall this month?

   B: Actually, I haven't gone at all. Why don't we go
      later today?

Keanu Reeves

3 Already *and* yet

A Check (✓) the things you've done. Put an ✗ next to the things you haven't done.

getting married

1. _____ graduated from high school

2. _____ opened an e-mail account

3. _____ gone abroad

4. _____ been in an airplane

5. _____ tried skiing

6. _____ gotten married

B Write sentences about each thing in part A. Use *already* and *yet*.

> **Grammar note: Already *and* yet**
>
> **Already** *is used in positive statements with the present perfect.*
> I've **already** graduated from high school.
>
> **Yet** *is used in negative statements with the present perfect.*
> I haven't graduated from college **yet**.

1. _____

2. _____

3. _____

4. _____

5. _____

6. _____

4 *Complete these sentences with* for *or* since.

1. Damien has lived in Hong Kong _____ 2001.

2. I have been a nurse _____ several years.

3. Masayuki was an exchange student in Spain _____ a whole semester.

4. I'm so sleepy. I've been awake _____ 4:00 this morning.

5. Mr. and Mrs. Chang have been married _____ nearly 40 years.

6. Maggie has had the same hairstyle _____ high school.

7. How are you? I haven't seen you _____ your wedding.

8. Where have you been? I've been here _____ over an hour!

9. I haven't had this much fun _____ I was a kid.

5   *Look at these pictures. How often have you done these things?*
Write sentences using the expressions in the box.

I've . . . many times   I've . . . once or twice.
I've . . . three or four times.   I haven't . . . lately.
I've . . . several times.   I've never . . .

ride a roller coaster

1. _____

_____

go to a nightclub

2. _____

_____

go bungee jumping

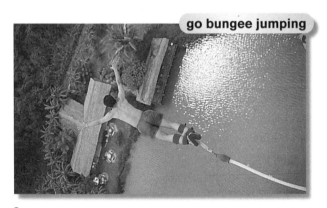

3. _____

_____

call home

4. _____

_____

see an opera

5. _____

_____

play tennis

6. _____

_____

6 Horror stories!

A Read these stories about two terrible days.

①

NO WAY UP!

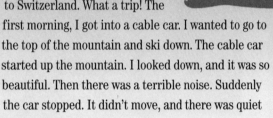

Have you ever been in a cable car? Well, I have. Last February, I went on a ski trip to Switzerland. What a trip! The first morning, I got into a cable car. I wanted to go to the top of the mountain and ski down. The cable car started up the mountain. I looked down, and it was so beautiful. Then there was a terrible noise. Suddenly the car stopped. It didn't move, and there was quiet everywhere.

It was cold, and it began to get dark and snow. I was alone for one hour, two hours. I thought, "They've forgotten me!" At last the car started back down the mountain. It went very fast. "Sorry," a man said when I climbed out of the car. "We've never had this problem before. Please, try again tomorrow." "He's joking," I thought. "I've had enough of cable cars for a lifetime."

②

NO WAY OUT!

I have always wanted to go fishing. Last summer, I went on a trip to Taiwan. On the last day of my vacation, I went fishing on a beautiful lake. Unfortunately, I didn't catch any fish, and I got bored. I decided to go swimming. When I stood up, my wallet fell out of the boat and into the water. It had all my money, my passport, my plane tickets – everything! I jumped into the lake to look for it, but I didn't find anything.

The next morning, I wasn't able to leave the hotel. I had no money to pay the bill and no plane ticket or passport to go home. So what did I do? I called my parents and asked for some money. I have never had such a terrible experience!

B In which story or stories did the writer(s) do these things? Write *1*, *2*, or *1 and 2*.

_1_	stayed in the mountains	_____	spent time on a boat
_____	lost a wallet	_____	waited for help
_____	enjoyed the view	_____	went swimming
_____	got no exercise	_____	had a terrible day

C Write about a terrible day you have had. What happened? What went wrong?

_____

_____

_____

_____

_____

7 *Look at the answers. Write questions using* **Have you ever . . . ?**

flamenco dancing

sumo wrestlers

oysters

wall climbing

1. A: *Have you ever watched flamenco dancing?*

   B: Yes, I have. I watched flamenco dancing last summer in Spain.

2. A: _____

   B: Actually, I saw a sumo wrestling match last month on TV. It was terrific!

3. A: _____

   B: No, I haven't. I've never eaten oysters.

4. A: _____

   B: Yes, I went wall climbing on Friday night.

5. A: _____

   B: No, I haven't. I've never been camping.

6. A: _____

   B: Yes, I have. I once rode my brother's motorcycle.

7. A: _____

   B: No, I've never been to India.

8 *Write your own answers to the questions in Exercise 7.*
Use expressions like the ones from the list.

> Yes I have. I . . . yesterday.   No, I haven't. I've never . . .
>   I . . . on Monday.   I . . . yet.
>   I . . . last year.
>   I . . . in August.

1. _____
2. _____
3. _____
4. _____
5. _____
6. _____
7. _____

9 **Complete the conversation. Use the simple past or the present perfect of the words given.**

A: _____*Have*_____ you ever _____*lost*_____ (lose) anything valuable?

B: Yes, I _____ (lose) my cell phone last month.

A: _____ you _____ (find) it yet?

B: No. Actually, I _____ already _____ (buy) a new one. Look!

A: Oh, that's nice. Where _____ you _____ (buy) it?

B: I _____ (get) it at Tech Town last weekend. What about you? _____ you ever _____ (lose) anything valuable?

A: Well, I _____ (leave) my electronic address book in a coffee shop a couple of months ago.

B: How annoying! Maybe that's why you _____ (not call) me for a while.

A: But you _____ (not call) me in a long time. What's your excuse?

B: I told you. I _____ (lose) my cell phone!

---

10 **Choose the correct responses.**

1. A: Has Marie called her family lately?

   B: _No, she hasn't._____
   - How many times?
   - No, she hasn't.

2. A: Are you having a good time?

   B: _____
   - Yes, in a long time.
   - Yes, really good.

3. A: How long did Joe stay at the party?

   B: _____
   - For two hours.
   - Since midnight.

4. A: How many times has Gina lost her keys?

   B: _____
   - Twice.
   - Already.

5. A: What about a tour of the city?

   B: _____
   - I've never, have you?
   - Sure. I hear it's great.

6. A: Have you been here long?

   B: _____
   - No, not yet.
   - No, just a few minutes.

11 It's a very exciting place!

1 ***Choose the correct words to complete the sentences.***

New York City

1. Prices are very high in New York City. Everything is
   pretty _____*expensive*_____ there.
   (cheap / expensive / stressful)

2. Rome is a beautiful old city. There are not many
   _____ buildings.
   (big / modern / small)

3. My hometown is not an exciting place. The nightlife
   there is pretty _____ .
   (boring / nice / interesting)

Rome, Italy

4. Some parts of our city are fairly dangerous. They're not
   very _____ late at night.
   (hot / interesting / safe)

5. Athens is a very quiet city in the winter. The streets are
   never _____ at that time of the year.
   (spacious / crowded / relaxing)

2 ***Choose the correct questions to complete this conversation.***

□ What's the weather like?
□ Is it big?
□ Is the nightlife exciting?
□ What's your hometown like?

A: _____

B: My hometown? It's a pretty nice place and the people are very friendly.

A: _____

B: No, it's fairly small, but it's not *too* small.

A: _____

B: The winter is wet and really cold. It's very nice in the summer, though.

A: _____

B: No! It's really boring. There are no good restaurants or nightclubs.

3 | *Choose the correct conjunctions and rewrite the sentences.*

Paris, France **Sapporo, Japan** **Marrakech, Morocco**

1. Paris is a very busy place. The streets are always crowded. (and / but)

   Paris is a very busy place, and the streets are always crowded.

   _____

2. Sapporo is a very nice place. The winters are terribly cold. (and / though)

   _____

   _____

3. Marrakech is an exciting city. It's a fun place to sightsee. (and / however)

   _____

   _____

4. My hometown is a great place for a vacation. It's not too good for shopping. (and / but)

   _____

   _____

5. Our hometown is somewhat ugly. It has some beautiful old homes. (and / however)

   _____

   _____

4 Check (✓) if these sentences need a or an. Then write a or an in the correct places.

> **Grammar note: A and an**
>
> **Use** a or an **with (adverb +) adjective + singular noun.**
> It has **a fairly new park.**
> It's **an old city.**
>
> **Don't use** a or an **with (adverb +) adjective.**
> It's **fairly new.**
> It's **old.**

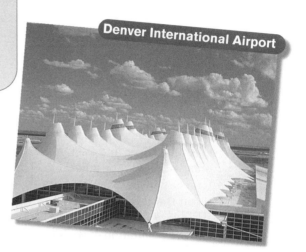
Denver International Airport

1. ☑ Denver has ^a very modern airport.
2. ☐ Restaurants are very cheap in Mexico.
3. ☐ Copenhagen is clean city.
4. ☐ The buildings in Paris are really beautiful.
5. ☐ Apartments are very expensive in Hong Kong.
6. ☐ Amsterdam is fairly crowded city in the summer.
7. ☐ Toronto has good museums.
8. ☐ Rio de Janeiro is exciting place to visit.

5 Complete this description of London with is or has.

Ever-Popular London

London _____is_____ Britain's biggest city. It _____ a very old capital and dates back to the Romans. It _____ a city of interesting buildings and churches, and it _____ many beautiful parks. It also _____ some of the best museums in the world. London _____ very crowded in the summer, but it _____ not too busy in the winter. It _____ a popular city with foreign tourists and _____ millions of visitors a year. The city _____ famous for its shopping and _____ many excellent department stores. London _____ convenient trains and buses that cross the city, so it _____ easy for tourists to get around.

6 From city to city

A Read about these cities.

Budapest

Los Angeles

Taipei

For many centuries, Budapest was two cities, with Buda on the west side of the Danube River and Pest on the east side. Budapest became one city in 1872, and it has been the capital city of Hungary ever since.

The population of Budapest is about two million, and the city is a very popular place for tourists. Visitors like to take boat rides along the Danube. Budapest is also known for its exciting nightlife. The best time to visit is the summer since Budapest is very cold in the winter.

Los Angeles was founded in 1781. With 3.8 million people, it is now the biggest city in California and the second largest city in the United States. It is famous for its modern freeways, its movie stars, and its smog. When the city is really smoggy, you can't see the nearby mountains. The weather is usually dry and warm.

Visitors like to go to the film studios and to drive along Hollywood Boulevard. There are some good beaches near the city, and Los Angeles is also close to Disneyland.

Since its founding in the eighteenth century, Taipei has grown to a population of 2.7 million and has become the cultural, industrial, and administrative center of the island of Taiwan. It's an exciting city, but the weather is humid and not always pleasant.

Taipei is also a busy city, and the streets are always full of people. There is an excellent museum that many tourists visit. It's a fairly expensive city, but not more expensive than some other Asian cities, so many tourists go to Taipei to shop.

B Complete the chart.

City	Date founded	Population	Weather	Attractions
Budapest	_1872_	_____	_____	_____
			_____	_____
Los Angeles	_____	_____	_____	_____
			_____	_____
Taipei	_____	_____	_____	_____
			_____	_____

C Complete the sentences

1. _Taipei_ _____ is cheaper than some other cities nearby.

2. _____ has good beaches nearby.

3. _____ was once two cities.

4. _____ were both founded in the eighteenth century.

7 *Complete these sentences. Use phrases from the list.*

☐ shouldn't miss ☐ can take
☑ should see ☐ shouldn't stay
☐ should get around ☐ shouldn't walk

1. You *should see* the new zoo.
   It's very interesting.

2. You _____ near the
   airport. It's too noisy.

3. You _____ the museum.
   It has some new exhibits.

4. You _____ a bus tour
   of the city if you like.

5. You _____ alone at night.
   It's too dangerous.

6. You _____ by taxi if
   you're out late.

8 *Complete this conversation with* should *or* shouldn't *and* I *or* you.

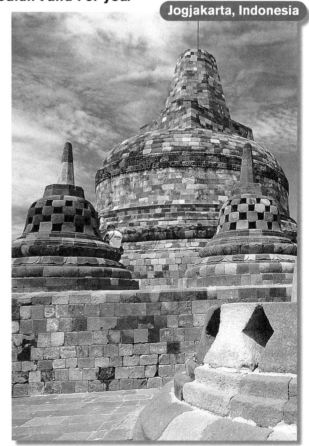

Jogjakarta, Indonesia

A: I'm taking my vacation in Indonesia.
   What *should I* do there?

B: _____ miss Jogjakarta,
   the old capital city. There are a lot of
   beautiful old buildings. For example,
   _____ see the
   temple of Borobudur.

A: Sounds great. Bali is very popular, too.
   _____ go there?

B: Yes, _____ .
   It's very interesting.

A: _____ take a lot of
   money with me?

B: No, _____ . Indonesia
   is not an expensive country to visit.

A: So when _____ go there?

B: Anytime. The weather's always nice.

9 ***Ask questions about a place you want to visit.***
***Use* can, should, *or* shouldn't.**

1. the time to visit

   What time of year should you visit?

2. things to see and do there

   _____

3. things not to do

   _____

4. special foods to try

   _____

5. fun things to buy

   _____

6. other interesting things to do

   _____

10 ***Rewrite these sentences. Find another way to say each sentence***
using the words given.

1. It's a stressful city.

   It isn't a relaxing city. _____ (not relaxing)

2. The streets are always full of people.

   _____ (crowded)

3. It's not a very beautiful city.

   _____ (fairly ugly)

4. When should we visit the city?

   _____ (a good time)

5. You really should visit the weekend market.

   _____ (not miss)

12 It really works!

1 Any suggestions?

A Check (✓) the best advice for each health problem.

1. a backache
- ✓ use a heating pad
- ☐ get some exercise
- ☐ drink herbal tea

2. a headache
- ☐ take some vitamin C
- ☐ take some aspirin
- ☐ take a cough drop

3. a bad cold
- ☐ see a dentist
- ☐ go to bed and rest
- ☐ go swimming

4. an insect bite
- ☐ apply anti-itch cream
- ☐ use eye drops
- ☐ drink lots of liquids

5. sore muscles
- ☐ drink lots of hot water
- ☐ take some cold medicine
- ☐ use some ointment

6. a burn
- ☐ take a multivitamin
- ☐ put it under cold water
- ☐ drink warm milk

B Write a question about each problem in part A. Then write answers using the words from the box. Use the advice in part A or your own ideas.

| It's important . . .   It's helpful . . .   It's a good idea . . . |

1. A: _What should you do for a backache?_

   B: _It's helpful to use a heating pad._

2. A: _____

   B: _____

3. A: _____

   B: _____

4. A: _____

   B: _____

5. A: _____

   B: _____

6. A: _____

   B: _____

2 *Rewrite these sentences. Find another way to give advice using*
It's important . . . , It's a good idea . . . , or It's helpful . . . .

> ### Grammar note: Negative infinitives
>
> | *Problem* | *Advice* | *Negative infinitive* |
> |---|---|---|
> | For the flu, | don't exercise a lot. | For the flu, it's a good idea **not to exercise** a lot. |

1. For a toothache, don't eat cold foods.

   For a toothache, it's important not to eat cold foods.

2. For a sore throat, don't talk too much.

   _____

3. For a burn, don't put ice on it.

   _____

4. For insomnia, don't drink coffee at night.

   _____

5. For a fever, don't get out of bed.

   _____

3 *Check (✓) three health problems you have had. Write what you*
did for each one. Use the remedies below or your own remedies.

Health problems

☐ a backache
☐ a headache
☐ a toothache
☐ a cold
☐ a sore throat
☐ the hiccups
☐ a sunburn
☐ stress

Some remedies

take some aspirin	get some medicine from the drugstore
use some lotion	put some ointment on it
take some cough drops	see my doctor/dentist
go to bed	do nothing

Example: *Yesterday, I had a bad headache so I took some aspirin.*

1. _____

2. _____

3. _____

4 *Getting to sleep*

A How many hours do you sleep each night? Do you ever have difficulty getting to sleep? What do you do? Read the article.

Sleep

Most people need seven to eight hours of sleep a night. Some people need less than this, and some people need more.

According to sleep expert Dr. Robert Schachter, many people have difficulty sleeping, but they do not know why. Most people know it is important not to drink coffee or tea before they go to bed – both beverages have caffeine. Caffeine keeps people awake. However, not everybody knows that some medicines, such as cold tablets, also have caffeine in them. Stress can cause insomnia, too. Busy people with stressful jobs may not be able to sleep at night.

Dr. Schachter suggests, "You shouldn't use your bedroom as a TV room or an exercise room. You should use it for sleeping only. It's a good idea to have a regular sleeping schedule. Get up and go to bed at the same time every day. It's also important not to eat before bedtime. Eating may keep you awake."

And if all this doesn't work, try counting sheep!

B Check (✓) True or False.

	True	False
1. Everyone needs eight hours of sleep a night.	☐	☐
2. Caffeine helps you fall asleep.	☐	☐
3. Cold tablets can keep you awake.	☐	☐
4. Busy people may have trouble falling asleep.	☐	☐
5. It is a good idea to have a TV near your bed.	☐	☐
6. You should have regular sleeping hours.	☐	☐
7. You shouldn't eat just before you go to bed.	☐	☐
8. Counting sheep may help people sleep.	☐	☐

5 **What do you suggest?**

A Complete the word map with medicines from the list.

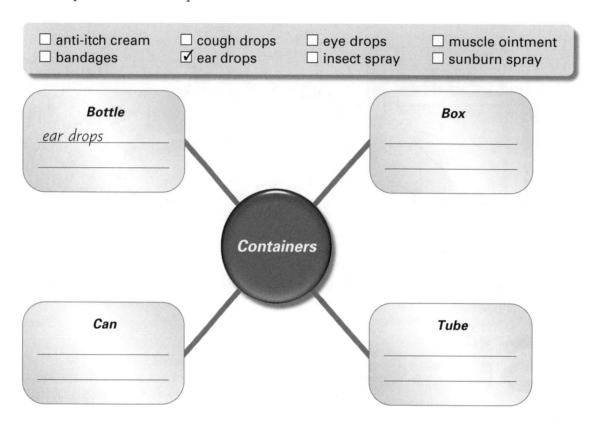

☐ anti-itch cream   ☐ cough drops   ☐ eye drops   ☐ muscle ointment
☐ bandages   ☑ ear drops   ☐ insect spray   ☐ sunburn spray

Bottle
ear drops _____
_____

Box
_____
_____

Containers

Can
_____
_____

Tube
_____
_____

B What should these people buy? Give advice. Use the
containers and medicine from part A.

1. Joe has very tired eyes.

   He should buy a bottle of eye drops. _____

2. Mary has a bad cough.

   _____

3. David has a terrible earache.

   _____

4. Andrew and Carlos have a lot of mosquito bites.

   _____

5. Manuel has dry, itchy skin.

   _____

6. Susan has a cut on her hand.

   _____

7. Jin Sook and Brandy got burned at the beach.

   _____

8. Mark's shoulders are sore after his workout.

   _____

Check (✓) the correct sentences to make conversations.

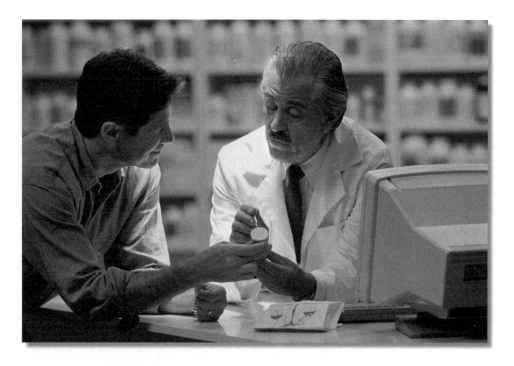

1. Pharmacist: ☑ Can I help you?
   ☐ Should I help you?

   Customer: ☐ Yes. Can I have a bottle of aspirin?
   ☐ Yes. I suggest a bottle of aspirin.

   Pharmacist: Here you are.

   Customer: ☐ And what do you need for a sunburn?
   ☐ And what do you have for a sunburn?

   Pharmacist: ☐ Do you suggest this lotion?
   ☐ I suggest this lotion.

   Customer: Thanks.

2. Pharmacist: Hi. Can I help you?

   Customer: ☐ Yes. Can I suggest something for sore muscles?
   ☐ Yes. Could I have something for sore muscles?

   Pharmacist: ☐ Sure. Try this ointment.
   ☐ Sure. Could I try this ointment?

   Customer: ☐ Thanks. And what should you get for the flu?
   ☐ Thanks. And what do you suggest for the flu?

   Pharmacist: ☐ Can I have some of these tablets? They really work.
   ☐ Try some of these tablets. They really work.

   Customer: ☐ OK, thanks. I'll take them. And you should get a pack of tissues.
   ☐ OK, thanks. I'll take them. And could I have a pack of tissues?

   Pharmacist: Sure. Here you are.

7 **Complete this conversation with the correct words.**

A: Wow, you don't look very good! Do you feel OK?

B: No, I think I'm getting a cold. What should I do _____ it?
   (for / to / with)

A: You should stay _____ home and go _____ bed.
   (at / in / of)   (in / of / to)

B: You're probably right. I've got a really bad cough, too.

A: Try drinking some hot tea _____ honey. It really helps.
   (for / of / with)

B: Anything else?

A: Yeah, I suggest you get a big box _____ tissues!
   (at / in / of)

8 **Give suggestions for these problems. Use words from the box.**

> Try . . .   I suggest . . .   You should . . .

1. I have a very sore throat.
   Try some hot tea.

2. I think I'm getting a cold.

3. I can't stop sneezing.

4. I don't have any energy.

5. I'm stressed out!

13 May I take your order?

1 *Show that you agree. Write sentences with the words given.*

1. A: I don't want fast food tonight.

   B: _I don't either._ (either)

2. A: I really like healthy foods.

   B: _____ (so)

3. A: I'm in the mood for Japanese food.

   B: _____ (too)

4. A: I can't stand spicy food.

   B: _____ (neither)

5. A: I don't like bland food very much.

   B: _____ (either)

6. A: I think Italian food is delicious.

   B: _____ (too)

2 *What do you think?*

A Look at the pictures. Write sentences about the food.
Use the expressions in the box and the given words.

useful expressions	
I love . . .	I'm not crazy about . . .
I'm crazy about . . .	I don't like . . . very much.
I like . . . a lot.	I can't stand . . .
It's a little too . . .	

greasy

1. *It's a little too greasy.*

healthy

2. _____

salty

3. _____

bland

4. _____

rich

5. _____

B What are your three favorite kinds of food? Write about why you like them.

_____

_____

_____

_____

3 Which restaurant?

A What kinds of restaurants do you like? Do you prefer a quiet place or a noisy place? What's important to you when choosing a restaurant?

B Read these restaurant reviews.

★★★★

Trattoria Romana is an excellent Italian restaurant. It has a quiet and relaxing atmosphere, and the service is very good. It's always crowded, so make a reservation early. The menu is not very big. There are only four entrées on the menu, but everything is fresh. The chicken with pasta is wonderful. Desserts are their specialty – rich and really delicious! It's a little expensive but very good. You'll spend about $25 per person.

★★

Last Saturday, I was the only customer at *Dynasty*, a new diner on 57th Street. It's not a good place to go. The waiters are slow and unfriendly. The atmosphere is boring, and so is the menu. The restaurant specializes in American food – mostly steak and potatoes, but my steak was raw and the fries were greasy. It isn't cheap, either. It cost me $22. If you go there, you certainly won't need a reservation. My advice, however, is clear and simple: "Don't go!"

★★★

Beirut Café is a great new Lebanese restaurant located downtown on the corner of 12th and Maple. The specialty is *meze* – lots of different small dishes, some with meat or fish, and others with vegetables. The atmosphere is lively, and the service is very friendly. There's live Lebanese music and dancing on weekends. Beirut Café is surprisingly inexpensive – about $18 a person, but you need to make a reservation. Check it out next time you're downtown.

C Complete the chart.

	Trattoria Romana	Dynasty	Beirut Café
Food	*Italian*		
Atmosphere	*quiet and relaxing*		
Specialties			
Service			
Price/person			
Reservation	☐ yes ☐ no	☐ yes ☐ no	☐ yes ☐ no

4 *Check (✓) the item that does not belong.*

1. ☐ iced tea
   ☑ chicken kebabs
   ☐ ice cream

2. ☐ seafood salad
   ☐ roasted lamb
   ☐ shrimp curry

3. ☐ beef burrito
   ☐ mushroom pizza
   ☐ cheese omelet

4. ☐ mashed potatoes
   ☐ french fries
   ☐ garlic bread

5. ☐ popcorn
   ☐ grilled salmon
   ☐ potato chips

6. ☐ sushi
   ☐ iced coffee
   ☐ hot chocolate

5 *Use one or more words to complete this conversation between a waiter and a customer.*

Waiter: May I take your order?

Customer: _Yes, I'll have_ the roast beef with mashed potatoes.

Waiter: What kind of dressing _____ on your salad – French, Italian, or vinaigrette?

Customer: _____ like French, please.

Waiter: And would you like _____ to drink?

Customer: Yes, _____ have iced coffee.

Waiter: With milk and sugar?

Customer: Yes, _____ .

Waiter: Anything else?

Customer: No, _____ . That'll _____ all.

Waiter: OK. I'll bring it right away.

6 Choose the correct responses.

1. A: Would you like fries or cole slaw?

   B: <u>*I'll have the cole slaw, please.*</u>

   - I guess I will, thanks.
   - I'll have the cole slaw, please.
   - Yes, please.

2. A: What kind of soda would you like?

   B: _____

   - I'll have a cola.
   - I'd like a hot dog, please.
   - A small order, please.

3. A: Would you like anything to drink?

   B: _____

   - No, thanks.
   - Yes, a hamburger, please.
   - I'll have chocolate cake, please.

4. A: What flavor ice cream would you like?

   B: _____

   - Baked, please.
   - Vanilla, please.
   - Ice cream, please.

5. A: Would you like anything else?

   B: _____

   - Yes, thank you very much.
   - Not at all, thanks.
   - That will be all, thanks.

7 Complete the conversation. Use the words and expressions in the box.

☐ am	☑ neither	☐ will	☐ can't stand them
☐ can	☐ so	☐ would	☐ favorite kind of food
☐ do	☐ too	☐ like it a lot	

Sherry: I feel tired tonight. I really don't want to cook.

Whitney: _____*Neither*_____ do I. Say, do you like Thai food?

Sherry: It's delicious! I _____ !

Whitney: I do, _____ . It's my _____ .

Let's call Chiang Mai restaurant for home delivery.

Sherry: Great idea! Their food is always good. I eat there a lot.

Whitney: _____ do I. Well, what _____ you like tonight?

Sherry: I'm in the mood for some soup.

Whitney: So _____ I. And I think I _____ have spicy

chicken and special Thai rice.

Sherry: OK, let's order. Oh, wait a minute, I don't have any money with me.

Whitney: Neither _____ I. What should we do?

Sherry: Well, let's look in the refrigerator. Hmm. Do you like boiled eggs?

Whitney: I _____ !

Sherry: Actually, neither _____ I.

8 Choose the correct words.

1. In a restaurant, the waiter or waitress takes your _____*order*_____ . (menu / order / service)

2. Baked potatoes are less _____ than french fries. (greasy / healthy / spicy)

3. Many people like _____ on their salad. (dessert / dressing / soda)

4. Some people rarely cook with spices. They prefer _____ food. (bland / hot / rich)

5. Vanilla is a popular ice cream _____ . (drink / flavor / meal)

14 The biggest and the best!

1 Geography

A Circle the correct word.

1. This is a stream of water occurring when a river falls from a high place.
   a. waterfall   b. ocean   c. hill

2. This is a large area of land that has lots of trees on it.
   a. desert   b. forest   c. river

3. This is a low area of land between mountains or hills.
   a. valley   b. river   c. beach

4. This is an area of water with land all around it.
   a. lake   b. ocean   c. island

5. This is a mountain with a hole on top. Smoke and lava sometimes come out, and it can be dangerous.
   a. hill   b. canyon   c. volcano

6. This is a dry, sandy place. It doesn't rain much here, and there aren't many plants.
   a. desert   b. sea   c. volcano

B Complete the names. Use words from the box.

☑ Canyon	☐ Falls	☐ Ocean	☐ Lake
☐ Desert	☐ Mount	☐ River	☐ Sea

1. Grand _Canyon_

2. Amazon _____

3. _____ Superior

4. _____ Fuji

5. Mediterranean _____

6. Angel _____

7. Pacific _____

8. Sahara _____

2 Write the comparative and superlative of the words given.

> ### Spelling note: Comparatives and superlatives
>
> | | Adjective | Comparative | Superlative |
> |---|---|---|---|
> | Add **-er** or **-est** to most words. | long | long**er** | the long**est** |
> | Add **-r** or **-st** to words ending in **-e**. | large | larg**er** | the larg**est** |
> | Drop **y** and add **-ier** or **-iest**. | dry | dri**er** | the dri**est** |
> | Double the final consonant and add **-er** or **-est**. | big | big**ger** | the big**gest** |

1. busy _____busier_____ _____the busiest_____   6. noisy _____ _____
2. cool _____ _____   7. old _____ _____
3. friendly _____ _____   8. safe _____ _____
4. heavy _____ _____   9. small _____ _____
5. nice _____ _____   10. wet _____ _____

3 *Complete this conversation.*
Use the superlative of the words given.

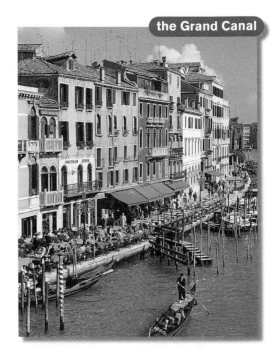

the Grand Canal

Ian: So where did you go for your vacation, Val?

Val: Italy.

Ian: How exciting! Did you have a good time?

Val: It was terrific! I think Italy is

_the most exciting_____ (exciting)

country in Europe.

Ian: Well, it certainly has some of

_____ (famous)

cities in the world – Rome, Milan, and Venice.

Val: Yeah. I had _____ (good)

time in Venice. It's _____

(beautiful) city I've ever seen. Of course, it's also

one of _____ (popular)

tourist attractions. It was _____ (crowded)

city I visited this summer, and there weren't even any cars!

Ian: I've always wanted to visit Venice. What's it like in the winter?

Val: Actually, that's _____ (bad) time to visit unless

you want to avoid the summer crowds. Venice is one of

_____ (cold and foggy) places in Italy in the winter.

4 **Complete these sentences. Use the comparative or the superlative of the words given.**

the Suez Canal, Egypt

Mount Waialeale, USA

Death Valley, USA

1. Canada and Russia are _____*the largest*_____ (large) countries in the world.

2. Russia is _____*larger than*_____ (large) Canada.

3. _____ (high) waterfall in the world is in Venezuela.

4. The Suez Canal joins the Mediterranean and Red seas. It is 190 kilometers (118 miles)

   long. It is _____ (long) the Panama Canal.

5. The Atacama Desert in Chile is _____ (dry) place in the world.

6. Mount Waialeale in Hawaii gets 1,170 centimeters (460 inches) of rain a year.

   It is _____ (wet) place on earth!

7. _____ (hot) capital city in the world is Muscat, in Oman.

8. The continent of Antarctica is _____ (cold) any other place

   in the world.

9. The Himalayas are some of _____ (dangerous) mountains to climb.

10. Badwater, in California's Death Valley, is _____ (low) point

    in North America.

11. Mont Blanc in the French Alps is _____ (high) the Matterhorn

    in the Swiss Alps.

12. The Pacific Ocean is _____ (deep) the Atlantic Ocean.

    At one place the Pacific Ocean is 11,033 meters (36,198 feet) deep.

5 *The coldest and the windiest!*

A Where is the coldest place you've ever been?

B Read about Antarctica.

ANTARCTICA is the most southern continent in the world. It's like nowhere else on earth. It's much larger than Europe and nearly twice the size of Australia. It's an icy plateau with the South Pole at its center. Antarctica is the coldest and windiest place in the world, even colder and windier than the North Pole. In the summer, the sun shines for 24 hours a day, but in the winter it's completely dark for about three months. Very few plants grow there, but there is some wildlife, including whales, seals, and penguins.

When Captain James Cook sailed around the continent in the 1770s, he found no one living there. Today, a few scientists work in Antarctica, but they only spend fairly short periods there. Many of the scientists in Antarctica are studying the ozone layer. The ozone layer is getting thinner and thinner worldwide. The biggest "hole" is over Antarctica, where the weather is getting warmer. Scientists think that this cold and lonely place can teach us a lot about the earth and how to keep it safe.

C Check (✓) True or False.

	True	False
1. Europe is bigger than Antarctica.	☐	☐
2. The North Pole is the coldest and windiest place in the world.	☐	☐
3. In Antarctica, it never gets dark in the summer.	☐	☐
4. There are a lot of animals and birds in Antarctica.	☐	☐
5. Captain Cook found a few scientists living in Antarctica.	☐	☐
6. The weather in Antarctica is getting colder and colder.	☐	☐

Geography quiz

Use the words in the box. Write questions about the pictures.
Then circle the correct answers.

☐ How big   ☐ How deep   ☐ How long
☐ How cold   ☐ How far   ☑ How high

Angel Falls

1. _How high is Angel Falls?_
    a. It's 979 meters (3,212 feet) tall.
    b. It's 979 meters high.

Australia to New Zealand

Australia

New Zealand

2. _____
    a. It's about 2,000 kilometers (1,200 miles).
    b. It's about 2,000 square kilometers.

the Amazon River

3. _____
    a. It's 6,437 kilometers (4,000 miles) long.
    b. It's 6,437 kilometers high.

Antarctica

4. _____
    a. It gets up to −88.3 degrees Celsius
       (−126.9 degrees Fahrenheit).
    b. It gets down to −88.3 degrees Celsius.

the Amazon Rain Forest

5. _____
    a. It's 6 million square kilometers (2.5 million miles).
    b. It's 6 million kilometers long.

the Grand Canyon

6. _____
    a. It's about 1.6 kilometers (1 mile) big.
    b. It's about 1.6 kilometers deep.

7 *Answer these questions about your home country.*

1. How big is the largest city?

_____

2. What's the wettest month?

_____

3. What's the driest month?

_____

4. How hot does it get in the summer?

_____

5. How cold does it get in the winter?

_____

6. How far is the nearest beach?

_____

7. How high is the highest mountain?

_____

8. What's the most beautiful town to visit?

_____

8 *Write the opposites to complete the crossword puzzle.*

Across

2 biggest
6 bad
7 shorter
8 worse
9 worst
10 near
11 lowest
13 driest
14 hot
15 shortest

Down

1 hotter
3 smaller
4 least crowded
   (2 words)
5 coldest
9 smallest
10 not famous
11 cold
12 best

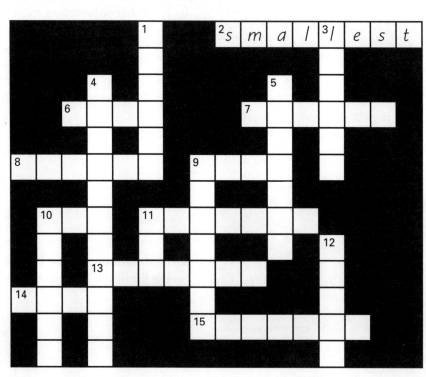

15 I'm going to a soccer match.

1 **Match the words in columns A and B. Write the names of the activities.**
(More than one answer may be possible.)

A	B	
☑ birthday	☐ act	1. _birthday party_
☐ comedy	☐ concert	2. _____
☐ dance	☐ fair	3. _____
☐ golf	☐ game	4. _____
☐ pop	☐ match	5. _____
☐ soccer	☑ party	6. _____
☐ street	☐ performance	7. _____
☐ volleyball	☐ tournament	8. _____

2 **Read Anna's diary, and write about her plans. Use the present continuous.**

July

Sunday	Monday	Tuesday	Wednesday	Thursday	Friday	Saturday
6	7	8	9	10	11	12
afternoon – go to Jeremy's birthday party	work overtime to finish the report	7:00 P.M. – see a play with Tony	night – watch the tennis match with Kate & Sam	12:00 noon – have lunch with Candy	stay home and watch the baseball game on TV	afternoon – go to the golf tournament

1. _On Sunday afternoon, Anna is going to Jeremy's birthday party._
2. _____
3. _____
4. _____
5. _____
6. _____
7. _____

3 Complete this conversation. Use be going to and the verbs given.

Marta: What ___are___ you ___going to do___ this weekend, Mark? (do)

Mark: I _____ to a rock concert on Saturday. (go)

Marta: That sounds interesting.

Mark: Yeah. There's a free concert in the park. And how about you, Marta?

Marta: Well, Brian and I _____ a basketball game in the afternoon. (see)

Mark: And what _____ you _____ in the evening? (do)

Marta: Brian _____ his mother in the hospital. (visit)

But I _____ not _____ anything really. (do)

Mark: Well, I _____ some friends over for a barbecue. Would you like to come? (have)

Marta: Thanks. I'd love to!

4 Choose the correct responses.

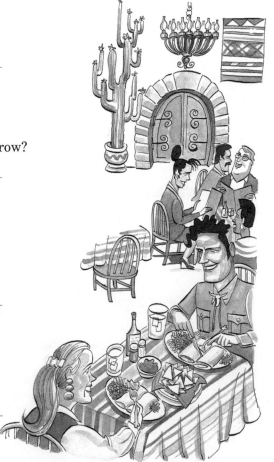

1. A: Would you like to have dinner at Rosa's tonight?

   B: _Great! But it's my turn to pay._

   - No, I'm not doing anything.
   - Sorry, I'm going away next week.
   - Great! But it's my turn to pay.

2. A: Do you want to visit the street fair with us tomorrow?

   B: _____

   - Yes, I'm going to.
   - Can we go to a late show?
   - Sure, I'd love to.

3. A: We're having friends over for dinner tonight. Would you like to come?

   B: _____

   - How about this evening?
   - I'm sorry. I'm working late tonight.
   - Yes, it would.

4. A: How about going to a movie on Saturday?

   B: _____

   - Oh, I'm sorry. I can't.
   - Nothing special.
   - No. I wouldn't.

5 *Write invitations to this week's events in Princeville.*

Exciting things to do this week in **Princeville**   All events scheduled to begin at 8:00 P.M.

Wednesday	Thursday	Friday	Saturday
Rock concert U2	**Amusement park** Lots to do for everyone!	**Musical** *The Lion King*	**Museum** Exhibition of modern art

1. *Are you doing anything on Wednesday evening? Do you want to see a rock concert?*
   OR *I'm going to see U2 on Wednesday. Would you like to come?*

2. _____

3. _____

4. _____

6 *Write about how often you do these leisure activities.*
Use the expressions in the box.

I often . . .
I . . . almost every weekend.
I sometimes . . . in the summer.
I . . . three or four times a year.
I never . . .

1. _____
2. _____
3. _____
4. _____
5. _____
6. _____

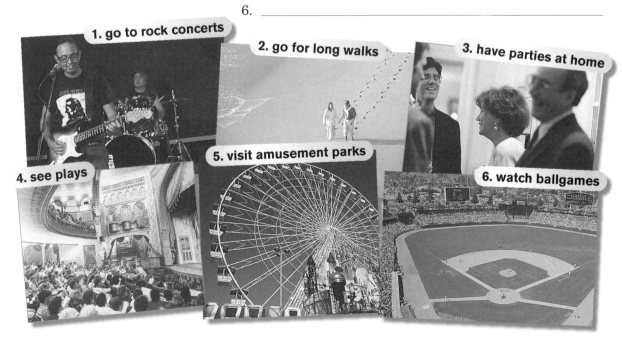

1. go to rock concerts
2. go for long walks
3. have parties at home
4. see plays
5. visit amusement parks
6. watch ballgames

A Have you ever sent or received text messages? Now read about them.

TEXT MESSAGES — *here to stay*

Text messages are short, typed messages of 150 characters each. The messages can include letters, numbers, and spaces. They are sent by Short Message Services, or SMS. This technology allows users to send and receive text messages on their cell phones. People can also send text messages from computers to a cell phone, and vice versa. This new way of communicating can save both time and money. And it's a lot of fun!

Text messages use a kind of "text talk" language. Words in text messages are often spelled the way they sound. For example, "Talk to you later" becomes "TLK2UL8R." When you abbreviate your words in this way, you can write messages faster. And you can fit more words into a short message on a small cell phone screen.

Text messages often contain emoticons. You can create these icons or small pictures with your keyboard. It's easier to understand them vertically, so turn your head to the left to look at these examples:

Incoming Message >>

B *I* U

TLK2UL8R

:-) equals "happy/smile"   ;-D equals "wink + big smile"   :-(equals "sad"

You can see this new electronic language in Internet chat rooms and in instant messaging. Have you ever received a text message but didn't know what it meant? Were you confused? Well, you're not alone. The more you use this new way to communicate, the better and faster you'll become at it. B4N (Bye for now) and BOL (Best of luck)!

B Can you guess what these text messages mean? Match each one with its meaning.

1. BBL _h_	**a.** I see.
2. ILBL8 ____	**b.** Where are you from?
3. CU ____	**c.** Laughing out loud.
4. SUP ____	**d.** Please.
5. ILY ____	**e.** I'll be late.
6. WUF? ____	**f.** See you.
7. IC ____	**g.** Thanks.
8. THX ____	✓**h.** Be back later.
9. LOL ____	**i.** What's up?
10. PLZ ____	**j.** I love you.

8 *Read these messages. What did the caller say?*
Write the messages another way using **tell** *or* **ask.**

For:	Ms. Tam
Message:	The meeting is at 10:30. Bring the fax from New York.

1. _Please tell Ms. Tam that the meeting is at 10:30._
   Could you . . .

For:	Mr. Alvarez
Message:	We need the report by noon. Call Ms. James as soon as possible.

2. _____
   _____

For:	Miss Lowe
Message:	The new laptop is ready. Pick it up this afternoon.

3. _____
   _____

9 *Look at the message slips. Ask someone to give these messages.*

> **Grammar note: Negative infinitives**
>
> | **Request** | **Message** |
> |---|---|
> | **Don't call** him today. | Please ask Jan **not to call** him today. |
> | **Don't go** home yet. | Could you tell him **not to go** home yet? |

Michael –
Don't meet me at the airport
until midnight. The plane is going
to be late.

1. _____
   _____
   _____

Lucy –
We're meeting at Dino's house before
the concert. Don't forget the tickets.

2. _____
   _____
   _____

Christopher –
The beach party starts at noon.
Don't be late!

3. _____
   _____

10 *Choose the correct words.*

Secretary: Hello. Schmidt and Lee.

Ms. Curtis: <u>May I</u> speak to Ms. Grace Schmidt, please?
(May I / Would you)

Secretary: I'm _____. She's not in. _____
(busy / sorry) (Can I leave / Can I take)

a messsage?

Ms. Curtis: Yes, please. This is Ms. Curtis. _____ you
(Would / Please)

_____ I'm staying at the Plaza Hotel?
(tell her that / ask her to)

The number is 555-9001, Room 605. _____
(Please / Could)

you _____?
(tell her to call me / tell her to call her)

Secretary: OK, Ms. Curtis. I'll _____
(give her / tell her)

the messsage.

Ms. Curtis: Thank you very much. Good-bye.

11 *Match the questions with the correct responses.*

☐ Yes, please. Could you tell him Roz called?   ☐ Let me see if he's in.
☐ That's OK. I'll call back.   ☐ My name's Graham. Graham Lock.
☐ Yes. My number is (303) 555-3241.   ☑ Yes, that would be great. Thanks.

1. Would you like to come to a party?

   Yes, that would be great. Thanks.

2. Could I ask her to call you back?

   _____

3. Who's calling?

   _____

4. Can I take a message?

   _____

5. Could I speak to Paul, please?

   _____

6. I'm sorry. She's busy at the moment.

   _____

16 A change for the better!

1 *Choose the correct responses.*

1. A: Say, you really look different.

   B: *Well, my hair is a little longer now.*

   - I moved into a new house.
   - I'm more outgoing than before.
   - Well, my hair is a little longer now.

2. A: I haven't seen you for ages.

   B: _____

   - I know. How have you been?
   - Well, I got a bank loan.
   - My new job is more stressful.

3. A: You know, I have three kids now.

   B: _____

   - Well, I've grown a mustache.
   - That's terrific!
   - Say, you've really changed your hair.

4. A: How are you?

   B: _____

   - I do more aerobics these days.
   - Well, actually, I turned 18.
   - I'm doing really well.

2 *Complete the sentences. Use information in the box and the present perfect.*

□ move to a new apartment   □ start going to the gym   □ stop eating in restaurants

1. Judy _____ .

   Her old one was too small.

2. Kim and Anna _____ .

   Now they cook dinner at home every evening. It's much cheaper.

3. Alex _____ .

   He looks healthier, and he has more energy.

3 Describe how these people have changed. Use the present or the past tense.

Shawn

Elena

1. _Shawn grew a lot._

2. _____

Susan

Eddie

3. _____

4. _____

4 Rewrite these sentences. Find another way to say each sentence using the words given.

1. Alice quit eating rich food.

   Alice eats healthier food now. _____ (healthier)

2. James lost a lot of weight.

   _____ (heavier)

3. Mary goes to a new school now.

   _____ (change)

4. Tess got divorced last year.

   _____ (married)

5. I've grown out my hair.

   _____ (longer)

6. We don't work out anymore.

   _____ (quit)

5 *Life changes*

A Have you ever . . . ?

- ☐ lost a job
- ☐ had money problems
- ☐ had trouble making friends
- ☐ worked in a foreign country

B Read the passages on the left. Then read the passages on the right.
Match the people's lives two years ago with their lives today.

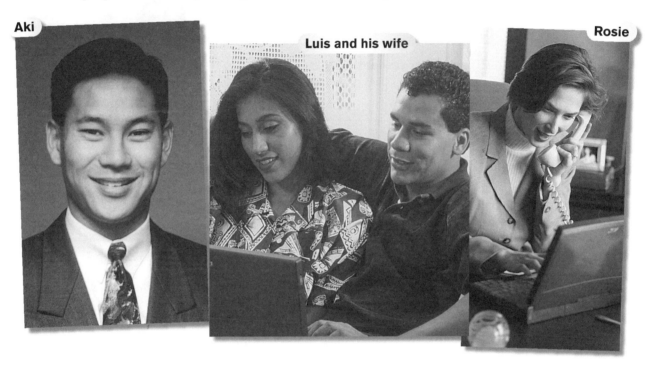

Aki

Luis and his wife

Rosie

Two years ago	Now
1. **Aki** Two years ago, I was a student, and I thought life was really good. I got up late. I spent the day talking to friends, and then I studied all night. I wore jeans and sweatshirts and had long hair and a mustache. I felt free. _____	a. Now my life has completely changed. I got married six months ago! My wife and I often have friends over for dinner. We're taking classes several nights a week. It's great! We're even talking about starting a family soon.
2. **Luis** I moved to a new town two years ago. My job was interesting, but I was single and I didn't have any friends. People at work were friendly but not very outgoing. We never did anything after work. _____	b. Now I work as a computer programmer for an international company. I've moved to Seoul and have started to learn Korean. Korean food is great, and I've gained several kilos. I feel much happier and healthier.
3. **Rosie** My life seemed to come to an end two years ago. I lost my job. Then I lost weight, and looked terrible. Money became a problem. I was very sad. I needed some good luck. _____	c. Now I actually look forward to getting up early in the morning and going to work. Of course, I dress up now, and my hair is shorter. But I don't really mind. At least my evenings are free!

C Underline at least two changes in each person's life.

6 *Complete the sentences. Use words in the box.*

☐ broke	☑ graduation	☐ responsibilities
☐ career	☐ loan	☐ successful

1. After _____ *graduation* _____ , Kirk and Nancy plan to look for jobs.

2. What _____ do you think you're most interested in pursuing?

3. I go to school, and I have a family and a part-time job. I have a lot of _____ .

4. Lucy wants to pay off her student _____ before she buys a car.

5. Marie lost her job. Now she's _____ , and she can't pay her rent.

6. I'd like to be _____ in my first job. Then I can get a better job and a raise.

7 *Complete this conversation. Use the words given.*

Melissa: What *do you plan to do* _____ (plan, do) this summer, Leo?

Leo: I _____ (want, get) a summer job.

I _____ (like, save) money for a vacation.

Melissa: Really? Where _____ (like, go) ?

Leo: I _____ (love, travel) to Latin America. What about you, Melissa?

Melissa: Well, I _____ (not go, get) a job right away.

First, I _____ (want, go) to Spain and Portugal.

Leo: Sounds great, but how _____ (go, pay) for it?

Melissa: I _____ (hope, borrow) some money from my brother. I have a good excuse. I _____ (plan, take) courses in Spanish and Portuguese.

Leo: Oh, I'm tired of studying!

Melissa: So am I. But I also _____ (hope, take) people on tours to Latin America. Why don't you come on my first tour?

Leo: Count me in!

8 *Imagine you have these problems. Write three sentences about changing each situation. Use words in the box.*

1. I'm not interested in my job these days. I spend three hours driving to and from work every day, and I don't make enough money! I can't find a new job, though, because of my poor computer skills.

> I hope to . . .   I want to . . .   I plan to . . .

_____

_____

_____

2. I've become less careful about my health lately. I've stopped jogging because I'm bored with it. I've started eating more fast food because I'm too tired to cook after work. And I can't sleep at night.

> I'm going to . . .   I'd like to . . .   I'd love to . . .

_____

_____

_____

3. I just moved to a new town, and I don't know anyone. I never do anything after work. People at work don't really talk to me. I haven't had a date in about four months. And I never seem to do anything fun in the evenings.

> I'm going to . . .   I want to . . .   I plan to . . .

_____

_____

_____

9 Choose the correct words to complete each sentence. Use the correct form of the word or add any words necessary.

1. I need _____to get_____ a bank loan. I hope to buy a
   (open / start / get)

   house soon.

2. Heather's salary is much _____ before.
                              (low / short / high)

   She had to take a pay cut.

3. After graduation, Jack plans _____ for an
                                   (play / work / move)

   international company.

4. This job is _____ my last job.
               (outgoing / stressful / expensive)

5. Mel hopes _____ to a small town.
             (move / live / change)

6. William and Donna got _____ last
                          (engage / marry / divorce)

   summer. The marriage will be in April.

10 Advise people how to make changes in their lives. Use expressions like the ones in the box.

| You should . . .   You shouldn't . . .   Why don't you . . . |

1. I've gained a lot of weight this year.
   _____

2. My hair is longer, but it doesn't look good.
   _____

3. I've gotten tired of wearing the same old clothes.
   _____

4. I want to start a successful business.
   _____

5. I'm often bored on weekends.
   _____

6. I don't seem to have any goals.
   _____

7. I've finished this textbook, but I still want to improve my English!
   _____